W9-APO-302

AVAILABLE NOW
from Lerner Publishing Services!

The *On the Hardwood* series:

Atlanta Hawks
Boston Celtics
Brooklyn Nets
Chicago Bulls
Cleveland Cavaliers
Dallas Mavericks
Denver Nuggets
Detroit Pistons
Golden State Warriors
Houston Rockets
Indiana Pacers
Los Angeles Clippers

Los Angeles Lakers
Memphis Grizzlies
Miami Heat
Minnesota Timberwolves
New York Knicks
Oklahoma City Thunder
Phoenix Suns
Philadelphia 76ers
Portland Trail Blazers
San Antonio Spurs
Utah Jazz
Washington Wizards

Hoop City   Long Shot

Basketball fans: *don't miss these hoops books from MVP's wing-man, Scobre Educational.*

These titles, and many others, are available at www.scobre.com.

To Order • www.lernerbooks.com • 800-328-4929 • fax 800-332-1132

ON THE HARDWOOD

PHOENIX SUNS

ZACH WYNER

On the Hardwood: Phoenix Suns

MVP Books
2255 Calle Clara
La Jolla, CA 92037

MVP Books is an imprint of Scobre Educational, a division of Book Buddy Digital Media, Inc.,
42982 Osgood Road, Fremont, CA 94539

MVP Books publications may be purchased for
educational, business, or sales promotional use.

Cover and layout design by Jana Ramsay
Copyedited by Susan Sylvia
Photos by Getty Images

ISBN: 978-1-61570-922-9 (Library Binding)
ISBN: 978-1-61570-921-2 (Soft Cover)

TABLE OF CONTENTS

Chapter 1
VALLEY OF THE SUNS

The Phoenix Suns were never supposed to exist. Phoenix was too small a market. And besides, what place did basketball have in the desert? Arizona was a place where baseball teams went for spring training and the elderly went to retire; a sunshine state where warm weather enticed people outdoors while most of the country bundled up, shoveled snow from their driveways, and scraped ice off of their car's windshield. Basketball was played in gymnasiums during those cold months. In the warmer months, it was played from dawn 'til dusk in the urban parks of Chicago, Oakland, and New York, or the rural settings

of Indiana and Kentucky. It was played in places where winters were cold and summers weren't so hot that the asphalt melted the soles of your shoes. Phoenix and basketball?

The saguaro cactus watches over the Valley of the Sun.

Before coming to Phoenix in 1968, Jerry Colangelo was the Marketing Director for the Chicago Bulls.

worried that a professional basketball team there would lose money. However, when a determined group of businessmen hounded the league to change their mind, the NBA relented. In 1968, they allowed the Suns to pay the $2 million entry fee and a new hoops cornerstone was established in the desert.

At the time, few people besides general manager Jerry Colangelo and Phoenix's first coach, Johnny "Red" Kerr, anticipated that the Phoenix Suns would become one of the NBA's marquee franchises. But through a combination of savvy drafting and outstanding coaching, it didn't take long for the Suns to

In the 1960s, this idea sounded about as far fetched as Phoenix and ice hockey sounded in the 1990s when the Winnipeg Jets up and moved from Canada to become the Phoenix Coyotes.

Despite Phoenix's proximity to west coast teams, the NBA

start holding their own against Western Conference foes.

In the 1968 Expansion Draft, the Phoenix Suns selected Gail Goodrich and Dick Van Arsdale. While Goodrich would only spend two years in a Suns' uniform, Van Arsdale would spend the rest of his career wearing the Arizona purple and orange. That year, while the country struggled through some of its toughest times, the Suns struggled to win, going just 16-66. It was a rocky beginning for the young franchise, but things were about to start looking up. The same could not be said for the United States.

The late 1960s were

a tumultuous time in America. The country was engaged in an unpopular war in Vietnam, and protestors nationwide were clashing with police in a hard-fought struggle

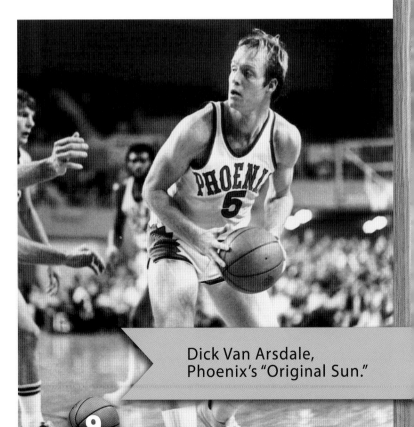

Dick Van Arsdale, Phoenix's "Original Sun."

In June of 1967, Muhammad Ali was stripped of his title for refusing to fight in the Vietnam War.

for civil rights. Taking hold of the baton passed to them by Jackie Robinson and Babe Didrikson, athletes like Heavyweight World Champion Muhammed Ali and 11-time NBA Champion Bill Russell were outspoken in their opposition to the war. They demonstrated the power that athletes have to affect change in American society.

This was the era into which the Suns were born. Phoenix, a town better known for its golf courses, retirement communities, and military bases, was not exactly at the center of the turmoil. But times change. No matter how quiet and peaceful a life you like to lead, turmoil has a way of finding you. A day would come when the Suns would be at the front of the pack, speaking out in support of the people of their community. But before growing into an organization that would take a public stand for civil

Muhammed Ali walks the streets of New York after being stripped of his title for draft evasion.

liberties, the Suns needed to grow into something else—a winning team. That first winning team arrived in 1969 with a 27-year-old rookie known as "The Hawk."

Connie Hawkins spent some of his best years playing for the Harlem Globetrotters and the ABA's Pittsburgh Pipers before finally being drafted by the Phoenix Suns. Upon his arrival in the NBA, "The Hawk" led the Suns in scoring for four straight years. Unfortunately for Phoenix, the NBA was having trouble deciding on a fair playoff system. In the 1970-71 and 1971-72 seasons, the Suns finished with 48 and then 49 wins. However, because of how they placed in their division, teams with

Connie Hawkins was the Suns' first All-Star.

worse records bypassed them and made the playoffs instead. It was an injustice that the NBA eventually corrected—but that correction did not erase the frustration felt by Suns players and fans.

After a 1972-73 season in which the Suns saw their win total drop,

Alvan Adams, the 1976 Rookie of the Year, rises for a jump shot.

"The Hawk" was traded to the Los Angeles Lakers and the Suns began the process of rebuilding. The term "rebuilding" is usually a signal to the fans that things are going to get worse for a time before they get better. It means that the veterans a team has relied upon to keep them competitive get traded for younger, undeveloped talent. Maybe it was the abundant sunshine, but in Phoenix, that young talent blossomed faster than anyone could have expected.

After two losing seasons, the 1975-76 Suns startled many by making the playoffs for the fist time in six years. Under coach John MacLeod, Rookie of the Year Alvan Adams and NBA champion Paul Westphal led the Suns to a 42-40 record and a #3 seed. The Suns were a balanced team, played solid defense, and shared the ball extremely well. In fact, they were so unselfish that seven different players averaged double figures in scoring. This kind of teamwork led the Suns past the Seattle SuperSonics and into their first ever Western Conference Finals for a showdown with Rick Barry and the reigning NBA champion Golden State Warriors. So far, the Suns had exceeded expectations, but nothing historic had happened. Sportswriters predicted that the Suns would fall to the Warriors and the NBA Finals would feature two powerhouse teams—the Warriors and the Boston Celtics. But as the saying goes, that's why they play the games.

Alvan Adams attempts to block the shot of Paul Silas.

The 1976 Western Conference Finals were even through four games. But in Game 5, the NBA Champion Golden State Warriors put up 40 points in the first quarter and cruised to an easy 111-95 victory. The Suns seemed to be setting. There would be no shame in losing. The Warriors had the league's best defense and they were number two in scoring. The fact that the Suns had managed to keep pace with the champions for four games was a victory in itself, right? Not according to the Suns' guards. In Game 6, they came out blazing. Keith Erickson and Ricky Sobers each scored over 20 points to complement Westphal and Adams' strong play, and the Suns edged the Warriors 105-104 to force a seventh and deciding game.

Despite the Suns nail-biting

victory, few gave them much chance in Game 7. With a regular season home record of 36-5, the Warriors had been nearly unbeatable. But the Suns hadn't come this far just to fade away. Down six points at halftime, they came out and put the clamps on

Paul Westphal helps the Suns achieve a narrow Game 6 victory.

the Warriors' offense, holding them to just 38 second-half points. It was time to celebrate in Arizona. The young Suns had brought the NBA Finals to Phoenix.

In their eighth year in existence, the Phoenix Suns were trying to announce their greatness to the nation. In the NBA Finals they encountered an opponent that had established their greatness time and again. The Boston Celtics, already winners of 12 titles (including eight straight from 1958 to 1966), were the most celebrated team in league history. This loaded Celtics squad included Hall of Famers John Havlicek and Dave Cowens, as well as perennial All-Stars Jo Jo White and Charlie Scott. In addition, they had home court advantage—something they utilized from the get-go.

Games 1 and 2 were no contest. With the Suns losing such one-sided games, many thought the series would be a

Charlie Scott spent some of the best years of his career in a Phoenix Suns' uniform.

sweep. Those skeptics clearly hadn't been paying attention. All season long, no matter what kind of a hole the Suns found themselves in, they dug themselves out. In winning Games 3 and 4 at home, they did it again. The Suns returned to Boston for a monumental Game 5, a game that to this day is considered one of the very best ever played.

In Game 5, the Celtics opened up a huge 34-14 lead behind the play of their stars. Gradually, Perry, Heard, Adams, Westphal, and Sobers chipped away at the lead. By the end of the 3rd quarter, the 20-point deficit had been cut to five, and when Paul Westphal converted a three-point play late in

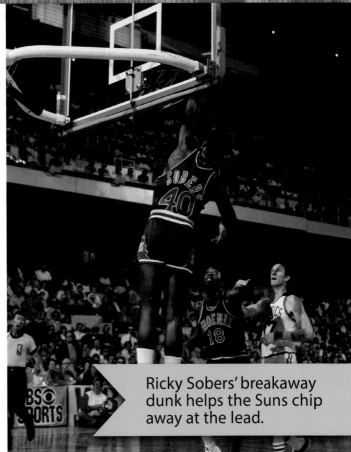

Ricky Sobers' breakaway dunk helps the Suns chip away at the lead.

the fourth quarter, the game was tied. The first overtime ended in another tie. It was in the second overtime that this game became the stuff of legend.

Inhospitable Arena
The Boston Garden had no air conditioning. On particularly hot days, oxygen tanks were provided to exhausted players.

Gar Heard leaps above the crowd to collect the rebound.

celebrate. Then with fifteen seconds remaining, Dick Van Arsdale hit a jump shot to cut the lead to one. The Celtics took the ball out, Westphal darted to the corner and stole the inbounds pass. He fed the ball to Curtis Perry, who missed a jumper from the wing, then tracked down his own rebound and launched a second jumper from between two Celtics defenders. The shot went down. The crowd went silent. With five seconds left in double overtime, the Suns had a one-point lead.

With 19 seconds left and the Celtics up by a point, Jo Jo White streaked to the basket and converted a lay-up to put the Celtics up by three. Sensing victory, the crowd began to

Down by three, with nineteen seconds left, the Suns had risen from the dead. Now it was Boston's turn. With five seconds to go, John Havlicek

Prodigal Sun Returns

Paul Westphal became an NBA champion in just his second year in the league as a member of the Boston Celtics.

took the inbounds pass at midcourt, drove to the wing and banked in a running jumper. The jubilant Boston crowd stormed the court. Celtics players fled down the tunnel and into their locker room. But the replay clearly showed that there was one second left on the clock when Havlicek's shot went through the basket.

It took some time, but the floor was eventually cleared. The Phoenix Suns called timeout. A timeout they didn't have. This earned them a technical foul. The Celtics hit the technical free throw, putting them up two. Why had Suns coach John Macleod done such a thing? Because he knew that with just over a second left, there was no way the Suns could get a good shot if forced to inbound from beneath their own basket. The technical had put the Celtics up two, but now the Suns had the ball at midcourt.

John Havlicek banks home a leaning jump shot to put the Celtics up a single point.

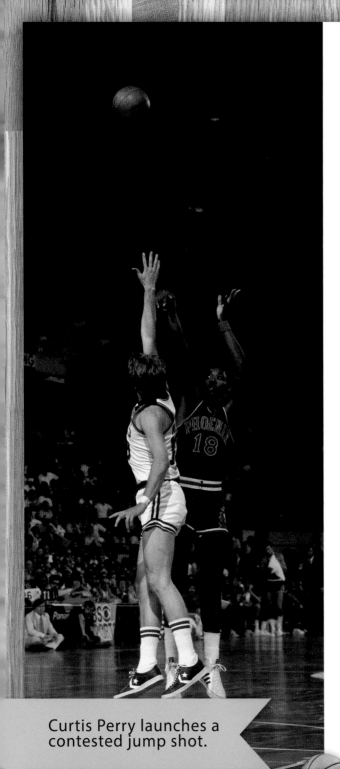

Curtis Perry launches a contested jump shot.

Curtis Perry threw the ball to Gar Heard near the top of the key. Heard pivoted, jumped, and released. The shot arced high through the air, the buzzer sounded, and the ball rattled through the basket. The second overtime was over; once again, the game was tied. Incredibly, the Celtics and Suns were headed to the NBA Finals' first triple-overtime game.

Despite a series of whirling jump shots by Paul Westphal, the third overtime belonged to the Celtics, who hung on to win the game 128-126. Two days later, the Suns fell in Game 6. Losing on their home court was a tough way to end the season, but no one denied that in the 1976 NBA Finals, the Suns had played like champions.

Following the 1976 Finals,

winning basketball became the norm in Phoenix. Led by three-time All Star/1984 Slam Dunk Champion Larry Nance, and Suns all-time leading scorer "The Man With The Velvet Touch" Walter Davis, the Suns made the playoffs eight straight times. However, by the 1986-87 season, the Suns winning ways had begun to deteriorate. For two straight seasons they finished on the outside of the playoff picture. Phoenix fans patiently awaited the player who might lead them back to prominence.

The first of those players arrived in 1988 in an unassuming 6'1",

High Flier and Denier

A three-time All-Star and winner of the 1984 Slam Dunk Contest, Larry Nance retired with the most blocked shots of any non-center in NBA history.

180-pound frame. He went by the initials "KJ."

Walter Davis averaged over 20 points per game six times as a member of the Suns.

Chapter 3
PHOENIX RISING

The rebirth of the Suns was nearly as swift as their decline. However, it's important to note that it almost didn't happen. In 1987, the Phoenix Suns nearly picked up and left town when Arizona's new governor Evan Mecham cancelled MLK Day. Mecham's decision not to honor Martin Luther King, Jr. and observe the national holiday upset many people, and owner Richard Bloch considered moving the team to Anaheim or Toronto. However, when the team's original general manager Jerry Colangelo swooped in and bought the Suns, the possibility of moving came to an abrupt end. Colangelo

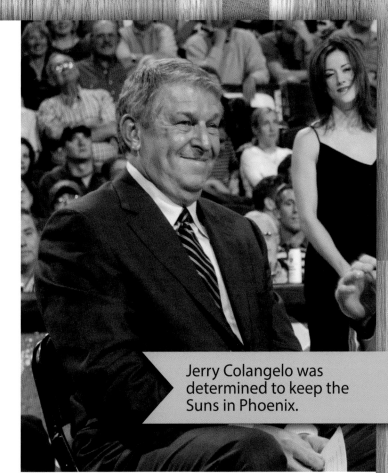

Jerry Colangelo was determined to keep the Suns in Phoenix.

had worked too hard to solidify Phoenix's standing as a basketball city. While the governor's decision to cancel MLK Day may have placed him on the wrong side of history, that mistake could be corrected. Moving the Suns would be permanent.

During the ensuing season,

the Suns struggled. Colangelo and general manager Cotton Fitzsimmons felt that the Suns needed to show dramatic improvement quickly. If the team could regain its consistency, and if its great fans would start buying tickets again, the NBA would likely stop pressuring them to move. However, in order to accomplish this, a big change was needed. That big change came in the form of a blockbuster trade that sent All-Star Larry Nance to Cleveland while the Suns acquired Kevin Johnson, Ty Corbin, Mark West, and draft picks from the Cavaliers.

Born in Sacramento, Kevin Johnson lost his father when he was three years old and was raised by his grandparents. At Sacramento High School, Kevin starred in baseball and basketball, and by the time he graduated from the University of California Berkeley, he was the Golden Bears' all-time leader in scoring, assists and steals. His play revealed a drive and determination that has

KJ tears up the PAC 10 as a member of the California Golden Bears.

served him well as a player and as a public servant. On the court, KJ was a lightning quick guard who could break down a defense with his ball handling, outside shooting and precision passing. Since retiring, he has worked hard to improve public education, and in 2008, he became the first black mayor of Sacramento.

In the 1988-89 season, the reins of the Phoenix Suns offense were turned over to 22-year-old KJ. At just 6'1" and 180 pounds, the little point guard loomed large, erasing any doubts about his ability—and making Colangelo and his new coach, Cotton Fitzsimmons, look like a pair of basketball geniuses. In just his second year in the league, KJ put himself in

Recurring Coach
In 1988, Cotton Fitzsimmons was entering his second stint as coach of the Phoenix Suns, having previously coached them from 1970 to 1972.

historic company, becoming the third player in NBA history (alongside only Magic Johnson and Isaiah Thomas) to average over 20 points and 12 assists per game. By season's end he had earned the NBA's Most Improved Player Award. He had

Kevin Johnson became mayor of Sacramento in 2008 and won reelection in 2012.

Majerle attempts to shoot over the NBA's all-time blocks leader, Hakeem Olajuwon.

future that had looked so bleak one season could turn around so completely by the next. Through trades and free-agent signings, Fitzsimmons and Colangelo had brought KJ all the help he would need to guide a high-octane offense. Joining him that season was high-flying All-Star power forward Tom Chambers, high-scoring swingman Eddie Johnson, sharp-shooting Jeff Hornacek, and rookie guard "Thunder" Dan Majerle. Come playoff time, KJ and Chambers would increase their season averages and Thunder Dan would emerge as one of the most dangerous streak shooters in the league.

also led the Suns to one of the most dramatic single-season turnarounds since the league's inception. One season after going 28-54, the Suns posted a record of 55-27. They were back in the playoffs, loaded with talent.

It seemed impossible that a

The 1989 playoff run would take the Suns all the way to the

Worst to First

The 1988-89 Suns turnaround of 26 games was the best in team history until the 2004-05 Suns came along.

Conference Finals before they ran into Magic Johnson's Los Angeles Lakers. In that series, the Suns were swept and some of their weaknesses were exposed. Over the next two years, few teams managed to exploit those weaknesses (Phoenix won 55 and 53 games), but the Suns were never quite able to beat the best. Without a post presence and consistent rebounding, they kept falling just short of their goal.

In recognition of their weaknesses, the Suns made another bold move. However, unlike the KJ trade, this move did not bring a group of unknowns to the desert. Nor did it bring a little man with big shoes to fill. Following the 1991-92 season, the Phoenix Suns brought a big man with an even bigger reputation

Charles Barkley led the 1992 USA Dream Team in scoring with 18 points per game.

to Arizona. As a member of the 1992 USA Dream Team and the Philadelphia 76ers, he had already earned recognition as a basketball royalty. He went by the name "Sir" Charles.

Chapter 4
THE SEASON

The 1992-93 NBA season was the finest in Suns' history. Never before had the team won so many games. Never before had they been the #1 seed in the Western Conference come playoff time. Never before had they done it behind the talent and leadership of a league MVP. The unit that was KJ, Tom Chambers, Thunder Dan, and Cedric Ceballos had been steadily improving for two seasons. When Sir Charles moved west, the Suns quickly made the transformation from contender for a division crown to contender for an NBA title. Many saw them as the team with the best chance to dethrone Michael Jordan and the reigning champion Chicago Bulls.

Born in Leeds, Alabama, Charles was one of those rare NBA talents who did not receive much attention during high school. He struggled with his weight, and did not even make the varsity team until his senior year—when a late growth spurt pushed him from 5'10" to 6'4". Although Charles put up excellent numbers that season, it wasn't until

Cedric Ceballos soars above the rim en route to winning the 1992 Slam Dunk Contest.

the state semi-finals that college recruiters noticed him. During the Alabama state tournament, an assistant coach from the University of Auburn reported seeing, "A fat guy… who can play like the wind." By the time he came to Phoenix, that "fat guy" was considered by many to be the second best player in the world behind Michael Jordan. By the end of his career, he would be one of just four players in the history of the NBA to compile over 20,000 points, 10,000 rebounds and 4,000 assists.

In his first season with the Suns, Sir Charles averaged 25.6 points, 12.2 rebounds and a career best 5.1 assists per game. His willingness to distribute the basketball reflected the Suns' unselfishness— an unselfishness that was clearly demonstrated when All Star power forward Tom Chambers agreed to come off the bench for this first time in his professional career. As a reserve, Chambers became

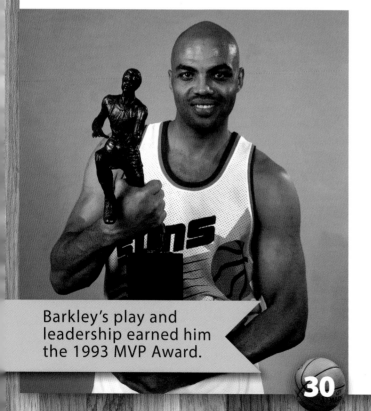

Barkley's play and leadership earned him the 1993 MVP Award.

the leader of a high-scoring second unit that included another long-time starter— the former shooting guard for the NBA champion Boston Celtics, Danny Ainge.

In the 1992-93 season, Charles Barkley led the Suns to an NBA-best 62-20 record. They won the Pacific Division with ease, and with their #1 seed in the playoffs secure, they rested their best players during the final four games of the season. This decision was one that former Suns great and current coach Paul Westphal would soon regret.

Coming off of the best regular season in team history, the Suns entered the playoffs against a #8 seeded Los Angeles Lakers squad

Four-time NBA All-Star Tom Chambers was named the All-Star Game MVP in 1987.

that they had dominated all season long. However, in the first two games of the playoffs, the Lakers' young center, Elden Campbell, outplayed the overconfident and out-of-sync Suns. Four games off had been just enough for the Suns to lose their rhythm. In a best-of-five series, Phoenix found itself in a 0-2 hole.

In the history of the league, no team had won a five-game series in which they lost the first two games at home. Coach Paul Westphal knew this when he stepped to the microphone for his post-game news conference and said: "We're going to win this series. We'll win Tuesday night, and then we play again Thursday. We'll win that one and then come back here and win, and everyone will say what a great series it was." It was a bold statement to be sure, but this was not a franchise that had gotten where it was through timidity. From their owners on down, the Suns had never backed away from a fight. Westphal made the guarantee. Now it was up Sir Charles, KJ, and company to win the games. They didn't disappoint. After winning a close Game 3, the Suns blew the Lakers out on their home court in Game 4 and then returned home to finish them off before an ecstatic (and relieved) home crowd in Game 5.

In subsequent rounds, the Suns dispatched the San Antonio Spurs and the Seattle SuperSonics. With 1.8 seconds left in Game 6 against San Antonio,

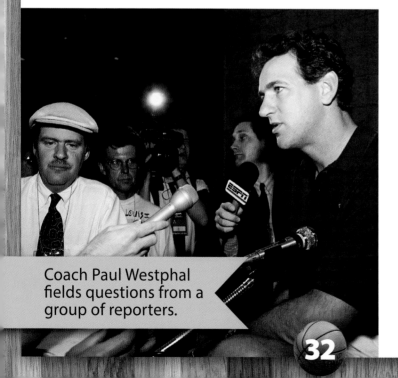

Coach Paul Westphal fields questions from a group of reporters.

Barkley's 20-foot jumper over David "The Admiral" Robinson sealed the series. Then in the Western Conference Finals, the SuperSonics stretched the Suns to the brink of elimination. Westphal made no guarantees this time. Going against one of the league's most explosive duos—Shawn Kemp and Gary Payton—the Suns had their work cut out for them. They won in convincing fashion. KJ, Thunder Dan, Tom Chambers, and Danny Ainge all contributed to the 123-110 win, but the biggest game was turned in by the biggest star—Barkley shined with 44 points and 24 rebounds.

In the 1993 NBA Finals, the Suns squared off against Michael Jordan's defending champion Chicago Bulls. Just as they had in the first round, the

Suns dropped the first two games at home. While Barkley scored 42 in Game 2, it was Jordan's 10 points in the game's closing minutes that sealed the victory. Following subpar performances in the first two games, KJ confessed, "No matter what anyone says about being ready, nothing will prepare you for the pressure of the Finals when you've never been there before."

Down 0-2, the Suns' season appeared over. It was one thing to come back against the #8 seeded Lakers. It was another to try and win four out of five against the champs. In order to win it all, the Suns would need at least two victories in Chicago

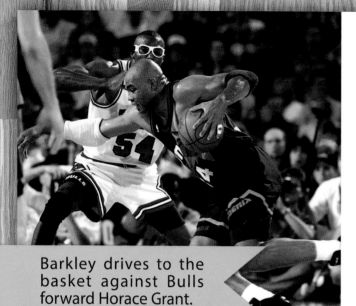

Barkley drives to the basket against Bulls forward Horace Grant.

to bring the series back home.

In Game 3 of the 1993 NBA Finals, the Suns played in the franchise's second triple-overtime finals game. With 18 lead changes and 12 ties, it was every bit as thrilling as their first. Michael Jordan and Scottie Pippen combined for 70 of the Bulls' 121 points, while KJ, Barkley, and

Exclusive Club
Barkley is one of only 17 NBA players to record a triple-double in the NBA Finals.

Thunder Dan scored 77 of the Suns' 129 points. Barkley called it the greatest game he had ever played in. When asked to rank it, Jordan smiled and said, "I can't say the best game I ever played in was a game I lost."

Barkley's Game 4 triple-double was not enough to overcome Jordan's 55 points. However, with the Bulls ready to celebrate their third consecutive championship, rookie forward Richard Dumas scored 25 points to lead the Suns to a shocking 108-98 Game 5 win. The series was headed back to Phoenix. If the Bulls were going to win another title, they'd have to do it on the Suns' floor.

Great games are remembered for a variety of reasons. The 1993

NBA Finals were chock full of great games, all of them memorable in different ways. Game 3 was remembered for its three-overtime drama, Game 4 for Jordan's 55, Game 5 for the inspired play of a rookie, and Game 6 for a single shot. That shot came with 14.1 seconds remaining and the Suns clinging to a two-point lead. Michael Jordan brought the ball up the floor and a quick series of passes found shooting guard John Paxson wide open on the left wing. Paxson hit the three-pointer and the Bulls won the game.

Following the series, MVP Charles Barkley said, "The great thing about the finals is we gained respect, and to do that is a great thing." One

Though the Bulls won the series, there many moments when Barkley frustrated Chicago.

group of people whose respect the Suns already had was the people of Phoenix. After the series, thousands of Suns fans demonstrated their devotion, braving scorching heat (105 degrees in the shade) to participate in a celebration of their beloved team. Jerry Colangelo, who won the NBA Executive of the Year for a fourth time that season, called the massive gathering "one of the most moving moments in our history."

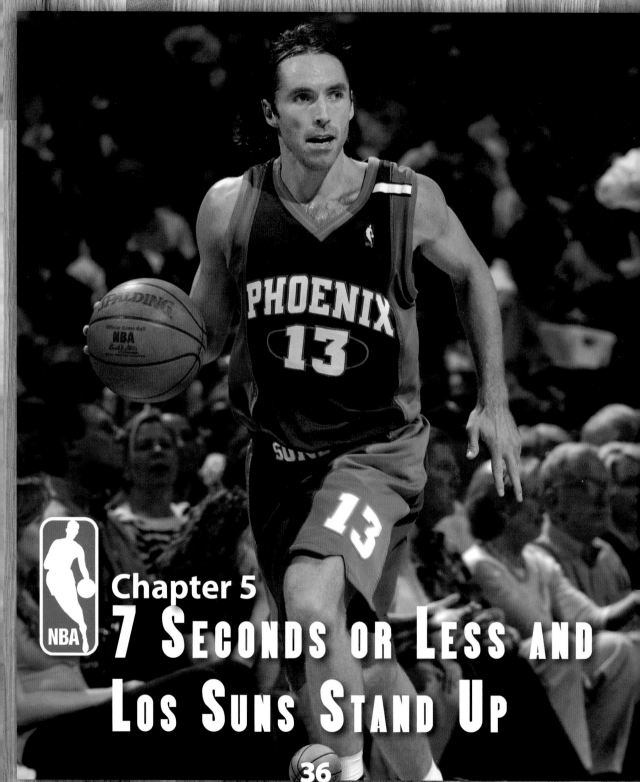

Chapter 5
7 Seconds or Less and Los Suns Stand Up

Over the next four seasons the Suns stayed relevant in the Western Conference, but they never quite regained the edge they possessed in 1993. The departure of Thunder Dan Majerle was a tough blow for both players and fans, and by the time the 1996 playoffs came around, the Suns had fallen far behind Seattle and San Antonio—teams they had beaten to advance to the finals a few years before. Following the 1996 playoffs, Sir Charles was traded to the Houston Rockets.

Featuring two of the greatest point guards of all time in KJ and young Jason Kidd, the 1996-97 Suns moved the ball extremely well. In fact, the KJ/Kidd tandem played so well that there was very little playing time leftover for the Suns' first round draft pick out of Santa Clara University, Steve Nash. The Suns made the playoffs, but were eliminated in the first round. While the next season saw Nash's minutes

Playing behind two of the NBA's best point guards, Nash struggled to get consistent minutes in his first stint with Phoenix.

increase and the Suns return to the top of the Western Conference, another early playoff exit convinced management that this group had reached its ceiling. Trades needed to be made. Among other moves, Nash was sent to Dallas for a trio of role players and a first round draft pick.

Consistency is the foundation upon which the Suns have made their name. No matter the expectations, high or low, this team has won lots of games nearly every year. This was true during Steve Nash's first couple of years with the squad, and it was true of most of the years that followed his trade to Dallas. However, in 2003-04 the Suns struggled, posting the third worst record in franchise history. Under new coach Mike D'Antoni, the team pushed the ball up the court and scored in bunches, but they were outplayed in all other facets

Steve Nash and Dirk Nowitzki were teammates and the best of friends in Dallas from 1998 to 2004.

of the game. Still, with young talent like Shawn Marion, Joe Johnson, and 21-year-old phenom, Amar'e Stoudemire, there was hope for the future. They were chock full of explosive athletes. What they lacked was a true leader, someone who

Mike D'Antoni has a sideline conference with Shawn "The Matrix" Marion.

could bring out the best in his teammates.

Born in South Africa and raised in Canada, Steve Nash brought a world of experience and intelligence with him when he returned to Phoenix. In addition, Nash brought an understanding that a team does not exist in a bubble. He returned to Phoenix determined to be more than just a teammate to the men he played with on the court—he was a teammate to Phoenix's diverse community. His positive impact can be measured not only by statistics, but also by statements made in support of Gay Rights, and against racial profiling.

Charles Barkley once said, "I don't believe professional athletes should be role models. I believe parents should be role models."

Steve Nash has proved to be a leader on and off the court.

and always will be. As a Sun, Steve Nash showed us the way professional athletes can uplift and inspire more than just a fan base; they can inspire people the world over.

In the 2004-05 season, Nash's on-the-court impact was as impressive as it was swift. The Suns staged a turnaround even more dramatic than the one Kevin Johnson and Tom Chambers engineered in 1989. The 2004-05 Suns tied a franchise record by winning 62 games, 33 more than they had the previous season. Amar'e Stoudemire earned the nickname "STAT" (Standing Tall And Talented) and the Suns earned the #1 seed in the Western Conference. While many doubted their ability to make

Charles spoke from his experience and wisdom, and he made a valid point. But thinking that athletes should not be role models doesn't make it so. They always have been

Born Again... Again
The 2004-05 Suns 33-game turnaround is the 4th best in the history of the league.

it all the way to the finals, the Suns had faith in their system. Steve Nash's precision shooting and 11.5 assists per game earned him league MVP, and coach Mike D'Antoni's "Seven-Seconds-Or-Less" offense (an offense designed to get a shot up in seven seconds) earned him the NBA Coach of the Year award.

Unfortunately for the 2004-05 Suns, their magical season ended in the Western Conference Finals against the San Antonio Spurs. But the Suns' elimination did not occur before they had won over legions of new fans. Steve Nash and Amar'e Stoudemire were now household names. During the playoffs, "STAT" averaged nearly 30

Amar'e Stoudemire dunks over San Antonio Spurs swingman Manu Ginobli.

points and 11 rebounds, while Nash dished out 11.3 assists and upped his scoring to 24 points per game. In Game 5 of Western Conference Semifinals against his former Dallas teammates, Nash had shown why he was the league MVP, scoring 34 points, grabbing 13 rebounds, and dishing out 12 assists. It seemed he'd reached his apex... that is, until Game 6 when, trailing by five with less than three minutes to play, Nash scored eight points in the final minute to seal the 130-126 victory.

Nash's subsequent years in a Suns' uniform were equally memorable.

Three more times he guided them all the way to the Western Conference Finals, doing it in 2006 (another MVP year) without Amar'e, who'd been lost for the season with a knee injury.

The 2007 playoff run may have been the most painful near-miss for the Suns and their fans. In the opening game of the Western Conference Semifinals against the Spurs, Nash cut his nose in the final minute of play. Trainers were unable to stop the bleeding and the Suns' captain and two-time MVP was forced to sit out and watch his team lose a close game. Later, with the series knotted at two games apiece, Amar'e Stoudemire and forward Boris Diaw were suspended for

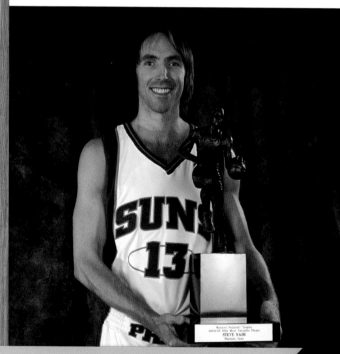

Steve Nash is one of 12 NBA players to win the Most Valuable Player award more than once.

Game 5 as punishment for leaving the bench when Nash was flagrantly fouled by Spurs forward Robert Horry in Game 4. The controversial rule that had been put into place to prevent bench-clearing brawls cost the Suns Game 5 and subsequently cost them the series.

The Suns could have used Stoudemire's help in Game 5 of the Western Conference Semifinals.

Nash's final postseason run in a Phoenix uniform came in 2010. The Suns had undergone changes in ownership and management off the court, and changes in coaching staff and players on the court, and they were expected to accomplish very little. But the 2010 Suns left a lasting impression that reverberates to this day.

In 2010, the country was three years into a recession. In hard economic times, people look for someone to blame. When you live in a state that borders another country, immigrants become easy targets.

Deadeye
In his eight years with the Suns, Nash shot 50% from the field, 40% from three-point range, and 90% from the line an NBA-record four times.

Steve Nash wearing a "Los Suns" jersey, showing his support of Arizona's Latino community.

it would make Latino members of their community targets for harassment and arrest.

Before the 2010 playoffs, the Suns announced that they would be showing their support for Latinos by wearing uniforms reading "Los Suns" on Cinco de Mayo. Nash was quoted saying that he believed the new law was "a detriment to our society and our civil liberites." Robert Sarver added, "We need to go on record that we honor diversity." Even Charles Barkley weighed in on the issue. In the pregame show on TNT before the Cinco de Mayo game, Barkley said, "Living in Arizona for a long time, the Hispanic community, they're like the fabric of the cloth."

The Cinco de Mayo game

Senate Bill 1070 was a law that made it illegal to walk the streets of Arizona without a passport, green card, visa or state ID. In addition, it required police officers to demand paperwork from people they suspected were there illegally. Steve Nash, Amar'e Stoudemire, and owner Robert Sarver took issue with this part of the law. They believed that was arguably the most important moment in sports in 2010. A pre-game three-thousand-person march outside US Airways Center proved this point. But the game was also an important moment in the Suns' season. It was Game 2 of the Western Conference Semifinals between the Suns and their arch rivals— the San Antonio Spurs. And as the game began, the Suns looked out of sync. Behind the play of All-Star Tim Duncan, the Spurs opened up a nine-point first-quarter lead. The Suns weren't playing much defense and the fans in attendance were oddly quiet. It was easy to imagine critics of the Suns' decision to wear the "Los Suns" uniforms saying that they had created a distraction, that basketball players should stick to the game and stay out of politics.

A young fan poses with his "Los Suns" sign outside US Airways Center on Cinco de Mayo.

Inspiring Foes

Moved by the Suns actions, Spurs coach Greg Popovich tried to get the team's "Los Spurs" jerseys for the game but it was too late.

Those naysayers would never get the chance.

On Cinco de Mayo, 2010, the Suns showed how much their community means to them. From the second quarter on, they played inspired basketball. They outscored, outrebounded, and outhustled one of the proudest teams in the league. Coach Alvin Gentry said he'd never seen his team play with such mental toughness. The Suns won the game by eight and kept that toughness going through the next two games, sweeping the Spurs and advancing to the Western Conference Finals. The fact that the Suns lost the 2010 Western Conference Finals to the Lakers in no way diminished what they had accomplished.

Before the 2012-13 season, Steve Nash departed for Los Angeles, ending one of the most thrilling chapters in Phoenix Suns and NBA history.

Nash scrambles for a loose ball.

But while the Suns struggled in their first season without him, fans need only look to the teams of the past for hope.

In the 2013-14 season, the Suns will be coached by their former All-Star, Jeff Hornacek. When asked how he plans to turn things around, Hornacek said, "I think... with Goran and Eric at the point guard, we have two guys who can get the ball and really go with it." The numbers support his belief. In 2012-13, Goran Dragic set career bests in points (14.7) and assists (7.4). Now Dragic will be joined in the backcourt by the explosive Eric Bledsoe. A star at the University of Kentucky alongside John Wall, Bledsoe's minutes have been limited in his first three years due to playing in L.A.

Going Vertical

In addition to running the offense, Dragic's 38" vertical leap allows him to finish above the rim.

behind Chris Paul. In the 2013-14 season, Suns fans will see firsthand why numerous teams around the league have attempted to trade for Bledsoe during his career. With Bledsoe and Dragic breaking down defenses, teammates Gerald Green,

Goran Dragic, initiating the Suns' offense.

Suns fans show their love for their team during a 2013 NBA Summer League game.

Shannon Brown, PJ Tucker, rookie Archie Griffin, and Marcin Gortat can expect to get plenty of wide-open looks and be on the receiving end of highlight-making alley-oops. Add the Suns 7'1" draft pick, Ukranian-born Alex Len to the mix, and you may have the beginnings of a revival.

Guided by the play of legends like Connie Hawkins, Kevin Johnson, Charles Barkley, and Steve Nash, the Phoenix Suns have been involved in some of the NBA's most electrifying games and fabled playoff series. One day they will win an NBA title. It will solidify their standing amongst the NBA's greatest franchises. But their reputation as fierce competitors and thoughtful citizens is intact, as permanent and unconquerable as the deserts of the state they call home.

11/16